fourteen poems

Issue 2

First published in 2020 by Fourteen Publishing Ltd, London, UK.

Design and typeset by Stromberg Design.
strombergdesign.co.uk

Printed by Print2Demand Ltd, Westoning, Bedfordshire, UK

ISBN: 978-1-910693-12-4

Hello and welcome to Issue Two of *fourteen poems*, the quarterly anthology of the world's most exciting queer poets.

When we launched *fourteen poems* earlier this year, we had the fear that no one would connect, no one would submit, no one would care. All too often we're told that there isn't an audience for queer voices, especially in something as niche as poetry.

However, the response from our readers and followers on social media has blown us away, with poets from across the planet engaging both digitally and through this very book you hold in your hands.

And we're so happy to say we've seen the same response in poets submitting too. This issue alone we have great poetry from London (where we're based), but also from South Africa, Greece, the US, Barbados (via Vienna!) and Ireland to name a few.

Our aim, as always, is to demystify poetry and to give voice to the diversity of the LGBTQ+ experience. Dip in and out as much as you want, taking the book with you throughout your daily life, or sit and read it cover to cover.

Poetry doesn't need to be stuffy, dry and accessible to a privileged few. It should be loud, messy, sexy, funny, angry. It should reflect our lives, our families, our friends. We hope you find your own reflection in some of these poems.

Enjoy!

Ben Townley-Canning
Editor

Instagram: @14poems
Twitter: @fourteenpoems

contents:

Mícheál McCann is from Derry. His poems appear in *Poetry Ireland Review, The Stinging Fly* and *Banshee Lit.*. His first pamphlet of poems—*Safe Home*—was published in July 2020 by Green Bottle Press.

Instagram: @mick_andsorts
Twitter: @micklemccann

Confirming What We Knew

We are lying together quietly as the night becomes morning
when you ask me where do I look for 'beauty'

(You hunch two fingers into a wrinkled rabbit to make
your sardonicism clear. An elfish smile in the dark.)

and I think your pleased sigh meant there was a simple answer
that had sailed over me while I sank into cartoon thought.

A six and a half foot lad with thighs as tight as harp strings
with a chest so firm, with rolling terrain to lollop down,

and the long train carriage of a penis, intimidating
and decontextualised, like a beech branch, lying on the path,

or the sorry yard just resting underneath this window
(my heart) that belches butterburs, colt's foot, open-mouthed trillium.

No difference, I reply, in the GAA fella and the wine-fade
shade of the weed that clambers through your gravelled garden.

You pause. And what when the coffee cup is empty, I say,
and stained along the blue enamel's rim? will beauty know

the twitch of my eye means *here we go…*, or where I am
at my saddest with all those glittering people around me?

Heaven is a garden, you'd say, and while roasting fragrant beans
I'd think, And what about all that time between now and then?

Mícheál McCann

Madelaine Kinsella is a poet based in Liverpool and a current MA Writing student at Manchester Metropolitan University. Her work is concerned with Scouse identity, fashion culture, female experience and queer identity, navigating bisexuality, exploring gender expression and how these things are perceived visually in a predominately binary society. Her work has been featured in *Bido Lito!*, *In The Red*, and she has produced work for the *Endyma Helmut Lang Archive*. She is currently interested interested in exploring Liverpudlian vernacular, and how much working-class femininity plays an essential role in that.

Instagram: @sackyourstylist
Twitter: @madskinsella

YOU TOLD ME YOUR EX WAS A MODEL AND I DIDN'T EAT FOR THREE DAYS

I'm not tall enough to ride. I could never be as poised.
I've never been poised. I'm heavy on my feet. I'm heavy.
Don't have square shoulders. Don't bring up the fact that
I did a photoshoot on my 13th birthday. Or my posed Instagram
feed. I know how that can sound antagonistic. I know how
that can sound runner up. I stack my achievements like a spine.

Like books balanced on my head. My balance prevents
them from staying and they sprawl on the floor like tampons out
a handbag. I hope she didn't see. The model. The fucking model.
Why did she have to be a fucking model? The closest profession
to fairy. Handler of ethereal portfolio. Delicate creature. I'm just
creature. Hunched and awkward. Stagehand. French bell ringer.

My accolades drag behind me like cans behind a wedding
car. Familiar to memory but no one takes notice. Like
tinnitus. Like not seated next to you. Like not the glossy bride.
Like chief bridesmaid of the 'you're-a-great-girl-but' wedding.
Like when you acknowledge the swan, why does the goose
seem to honk louder? I bet she was lovely. Really nice girl.

Madelaine Kinsella

Akpa Arinzechukwu is an Igbo writer dealing with their numerous identities. Their work has appeared in *Kenyon Review*, *Prairie Schooner*, *Trampset*, *Commonwealth Writers*, *Kanstellations*, *The Southampton Review*, *Sou'wester*, and elsewhere.

Instagram: @akpa_arinze
Twitter: @akpaah

Marvel

It is hard to believe
You startle me like this
Everyday
By kissing my lips
In the Park I thought we only admired
From a distance
My hairs standing in the sun
My body repeating your touch
Echoing its every sentiment
Taking its juice in as you work me
Through the Park, in the dark of the
Night, through to the light & we
Have a roof above us. Oh the miracle
It is, my hair dyed against yours: red &
Shimmering, me unable to mouth the marvel
Lets out a deep heavy moan & all the birds
Suddenly are born anew.

Akpa Arinzechukwu

Ayoola Solarin is a queer Black arts and culture writer, comics editor and reviewer based in London. She has written for *Dazed*, *VICE*, *Hyperallergic*, *Cause & Effect* and *gal-dem*, among other publications.

Instagram: @immortanayo
Twitter:@AyoSolarin

love scene, revisited (with only one actor present)

In this scenario I say "Valencia"
and you say
"yes, the wine. the olives! that
man who gave us
an extra scoop of *dulce de leche*
every morning,"
I smile slow and you follow
then say,
"who has ice cream at 10am?"
but you already know the answer–
me, the one in Valencia
still
tacky-mouthed; sticky fingered
from date scented dates,
doused with
spilled sangria that could do with
more wine and less *limonada*
not because it didn't taste like
a two year anniversary
made up of toothy grins
and warm skin
but because the sugar made us crazy–
crazier than two girls who
touched each other for the first time
not knowing that they'd have
tomorrow
not knowing they would make it
one week
let alone two years;
not knowing that five is the
cut off for crazy
after that there's just insanity,
and there's no excuse for that.

The peacock scarf
I wore that whole week
is hanging on the living room wall
still stained in places
from the oil in my hair
that we also used for the bread
on an evening when everything
turned the same hazy yellow
saturated finger nails
gleaming
lips sheened   slow drying   quick to part
lamps flitting streetside
before it's even dusk
I say "shall we go?"
and you don't say anything this time
just grab my hand
palms smooth and oilslick
everything coated in a lurid drizzle
my skin honey
molasses
I looked so good then
conjured up in brass-flecked irises
sugar-high
bare shouldered,
            -footed,
            -faced
I looked so *good* then
gold-rimmed, double haloed
a celestial
me,
the one in Valencia
still
with you.

Ayoola Solarin

Thomas Stewart is a welsh writer based in Edinburgh where he works as an English language teacher. *empire of dirt*, his debut poetry pamphlet, was published by Red Squirrel Press in 2019. He was highly commended in the Verve 2020 Poetry Competition and. His work has been featured at *Best Scottish Poems 2019*, *We've Done Nothing Wrong, We've Nothing To Hide* (Verve Poetry Press, 2020), *The Amsterdam Quarterly*, *And Other Poems, Ink, Sweat & Tears, The Glasgow Review of Books, The Stockholm Review of Literature, Oh Comely*, among others. His second poetry pamphlet is forthcoming.

Instagram: @tomstewart0808
Twitter: @ThomasStewart08

Three Grindr Poems

i)   Cardiff, 2013

I told you to call me
anything but   my name

the slut, the student,
the boss, boy

my anonymity is my authority

it means that
when I leave

you cannot
come after me.

ii)   Milan, 2014

You were beautiful,

strong enough
to pick

me up
and carry me

to the bed
you asked

to see me
again

so I

said no,

I wanted
to keep

you as beautiful
and perfect

as I knew
you could be

in my memories.

iii)   Edinburgh, 2016
(or story thief)

I am a story thief, a hustler,
come to your open door,
and find you
over the kitchen table

I unbuckle, do my part
feel the criminal
within me,
the blood pumping through,

as I hold your waist I think
of the poem
I'll write one day
about you.

Thomas Stewart

Rhienna Renèe Guedry is a queer writer, artist, DJ, and Tarot deck creator who found her way to the Pacific Northwest, perhaps solely to get use of her vintage outerwear collection. Her work can be found or is forthcoming in *Empty Mirror*, *Bitch Magazine*, *Screen Door*, *Scalawag Magazine*, *Taking the Lane*, and elsewhere in print and on the internet. Find more about her projects at rhienna.com or @chouchoot on Twitter.

sweat from the seam

find the ridge think of it like the
way a book lands open after falling off a shelf
                 it is rarely a halfway point
use a wide dull blade
the sharper the shucking knife the more risky a wrong turn
stab in at the point that is your best guess
you'll know you have it   when it breathes water
adjust yourself first then twist the knife like a skeleton key
clutch   the body of the thing in the palm
make nesting dolls of hands and shells
a little hallelujah of prayers for these damn blessings
                                  the angle just so
a crypt that creaks open on hinges
of moss and muscle it is an invitation
pour the liquor down the throat and suck the shallow
side where the blade lifts a perfect ribbon's   curl
your mouth and tongue you'll use them
to separate the hard from the soft

Rhienna Renèe Guedry

Anthony Aguero is a queer writer in Los Angeles, CA. His work has appeared, or will appear, in the *Bangalore Review*, *2River View*, *The Acentos Review*, *The Temz Review*, *Rhino Poetry*, and *Cathexis Northwest Press*. You can follow his Instagram or Twitter @ shesnotinsorry

His Profile Says He is Hunting

And I am immediately swept back to the time my
Tio Joe shot a pig in the head and all that blood had
Nowhere to run but into an unused bathtub tucked
Neatly in the far back of the land my Grandfather
Has owned since just after the war, a war, his war.
Since every war is something personal when you're
Placed in the middle of it all happening, blazing in
Your ear.

And I am immediately swept back to the time my
Same Tio guts the pig in front of our innocent eyes,
The same way that same man has intended for my
Body. The same body that has wrung itself in hopes
For a second chance. My war. My ears hot and
Blazing and waiting for what is wrong with my body.
He handles the pig's skin indirectly and impersonal.
Your skin.

And I am immediately swept back to the time my
Tio Joe didn't cry when he took this pig's life,
I wonder if every war begins with a man in hunt.
I wonder if he looks at my body and wonders the
Safest place to point the gun. I wonder how he
Defines the term *clean*. The meat, tender, falling
Softly off the bone. His personal vendetta, his war.
Your turn.

Anthony Aguero

Kostya Tsolakis is a London-based poet and journalist, born and raised in Athens, Greece. In 2019 he won the Oxford Brookes International Poetry Competition (EAL category). He founded and co-edits *harana poetry*, the online magazine for poets writing in English as a second or parallel language, and is deputy poetry editor at *Ambit*. His debut pamphlet will be published by ignitionpress in November 2020.

Instagram/Twitter: @kostyanaut

Vine

Gift from my forefather,
green calligrapher, tell me,
do your roots absorb
every voice cast
in this yard? Endless
Easter feasts, arguments,
the breaking of terrible
deaths. Each leaf you bear,
a word from an ancestor.
I pick them, fill them with
rice, mint, dill. My mouth
tastes sweetness. In tile-
searing heat, I sit
in your cool, watch
the black-and-white cat cling
to your fraying, twisting
bark like I cling
to our name – I,
your very last leaf
closest to the blank sun.

Kostya Tsolakis

Ben Strak's poetry explores queer life in cities and the natural world. He has been published in *Oxford Poetry*, *Magma & Frogmore Papers*. Last year he was awarded 3rd Prize in the Magma Poetry Judge's Prize, judged by Andrew McMillan and was shortlisted for the Frogmore Poetry Prize, judged by John O'Donoghue. He lives in South London.

Instagram: @benjaminstrak
twitter: @benstrak_poetry

Blood Beech

Perhaps we should have seen
your burned leaves as a warning
- aflame by the house in spring

when everything else greened
as it should have. Only your leaves stained
purple, as though bruised in their bud.

A freak, as children we ran round you,
as far from the summer dark
of your canopy as possible.

The words that, later, we scratched
with plastic cob skewers into
the thin bark of your trunk.

In this language you are called
copper, innocent as a kettle
of brewed tea, but in others

they know you as blood, a trace
of some old violence
in your rising sap.

I think of my blood rising,
the bruises that have bloomed
on this body in daylight

and in the dark at home unseen.
The crying out your crown has heard,
the rushing of sirens.

Perhaps I once believed
you were a curse, tree, but I see
what you have done with

the rare suffering granted
just to you, how you are tall
and ancient with it,

still uninterrupted.
I hear in your leaves instead
an injunction only to grow.

Ben Strak

Nkateko Masinga is an award-winning South African poet and 2019 Fellow of the Ebedi International Writers Residency. She is currently the director of the Internship Program at *Africa In Dialogue*, an online interview magazine that archives creative and critical insights with Africa's leading storytellers, as well as the founder and managing director of NSUKU Publishing Consultancy. She is the author of a digital chapbook titled *the heart is a caged animal*, published by Praxis Magazine. Her latest chapbook, *psalm for chrysanthemums*, has been selected by the African Poetry Book Fund and Akashic Books to be published in the 2020 New Generation African Poets chapbook box set.

to consummate

i used to think it meant
to consume one's mate,
like the praying mantis,
or black widow spider,

the way it hurt at first.
but we both survived
and lived to repeat it,
nightly some months.

i cared a greater deal
for the holding after
& the longing before,
our gentle beginning

being the image i held
as you unfolded folds
of skin, kneading me,
coaxing me to relax.

i want to try it all again
now that you have left,
the way i first imagined
it would be, safe & soft

like spring rain, rippling
waves & gentle rocking.

Nkateko Masinga

Dominic Leonard's writing can be found in *Poetry London*, *PN Review*, *Pain*, *The TLS*, and elsewhere. His pamphlet *love, bring myself* (Broken Sleep, 2019), was a Poetry Book Society Recommendation, and in 2019 he received an Eric Gregory Award.

Twitter: @le0nardpoetry

Dollhouse

There was a mother
who fell back,
assiduously. I'm
most people are
always worrying
it is so difficult;
the world or
the world is
not enough. No
one really is alive
more than I am
alive, secured
to the sot & thrall
of the hurling thing,
aloft on the bough
of me; the boy I'd
want to know
is a fraud, hurting
blue, as a star retains
its hidden crush –
his swallow
of dark, his frame of
burning, a lit hilltop fir –
o glory to the
ground where I can
make a locket of this
body, to keep it,
to be not here only.

Dominic Leonard

Georgie Henley is an actor and writer, born in Yorkshire and currently living in London. Her work has been published by *clavmag*, *Cipher Press*, and *Pilot Press*.

Instagram: @awkwardcrone
Twitter: @geohenleyreal

Blush

last night I met a girl
her smile was so wide
I dreamed she would
swallow me
a carnation in each cheek
I spread her sternum
ribs breathed heat
I have no heart only
hollow dragon husk
ravenous
I ache for what is golden
the source
I imagine how a bruise
a peony pressed
would bloom on her skin
fox blood in fresh milk
the hunger will kill me
before the thirst

Georgie Henley

Shon Mapp writes poetry and short stories that explore the physicality of cultural identity, nuclear kinship, and queer intimacy. Born in Barbados, she immigrated to the US at a young age. She moved to Vienna, Austria in 2019 with her wife. Inspired by the diverse artistic community in Vienna, she also creates mixed media art and ekphrastic poetry.

Instagram: @shon.mapp
Twitter: @ShonMapp

Citizenless

What of this hyphenated existence?
I do not accept either assignment
So they, push me into tight corners
And force me to stare
At the line where two walls meet
and disappear into themselves
unto themselves
Should I do the same?
Accept errant construction of who I am
becoming, a monolith
born of erosion and unconscious neglect
Enshrined in stone
Solitary and belonging to no one
Am I still not mine to define?

Shon Mapp

Evan Williams is an undergraduate at the University of Chicago. His work can be found or is forthcoming in *DIAGRAM*, *the Rockvale Review* and *The New Territory Magazine*, among others.

Instagram/twitter: @evansquilliams

The New Achilles

After Chen Chen's *If I Should Die Tomorrow, Please Note That I Will Miss The Particular*

I dump olive
oil on the butternut squash
singing aloud
the word *callipygian* how sexy
to have a well-shaped buttocks
to be callipygous sculpturesque Greek-beauty
glute-glamorous Gomorrah of the gods
here I am with this whole ass
bottle of olive oil emptied
over the curvaceous lumps of my squash
the oven is turned on
soon my bodacious butternut will come out
and all the Greek kings will
forget Helen.

Evan Williams